LOST TRANSMISSIONS FROM E.T. NUMBER STATIONS

LOST TRANSMISSIONS FROM E.T. NUMBER STATIONS

A Collection of Terrestrial Poetry

Benjamin Newman

gatekeeper press
Columbus, Ohio

Lost Transmissions from E.T. Number Stations:
A Collection of Terrestrial Poetry

Published by Gatekeeper Press
2167 Stringtown Rd, Suite 109
Columbus, OH 43123-2989
www.GatekeeperPress.com

Library of Congress Control Number: 2020948408

ISBN (paperback): 9781642375190

A Poem is a meditation.

This book is an experiment in love. Love for yourself, myself, and our enemies. This is a call to love with all our hearts, and peacefully develop and preserve a way of life worth living.

The world in which we find ourselves is much stranger than most would have you believe.

You have the ability to create incredible moments, all you need to do is suspend your disbelief, and listen with an open mind.

There is a subtle art to living.

The following pages may hold sadness, joy, hate, love, despair, hope, and anything in between.

Use these messages and thoughts as guides for contemplation.

Honesty is everything.

Love,
Schmuel.

A Cesspool.

.

.

What has changed?

.

.

If only the spiders
knew

.

.

to hang their webs by
our porchlights

.

.

where they'd always
be full.

She gave of a certain
strength,

.

.

a plush steadfastness,

.

.

That seemed to be
missing in most
people.

.

.

There was a certain
honesty about the
way he was assem-
bled which

.

made it seem as
though he had the
power to make
everything ok.

.

.

Between the trees
and the truffles,
.
.
the leaves twist and
shuffle,
.
.
while you lay in
peace.
.
.
Amidst the trees and
the breeze,
.
.
is cradled a skeleton.
.
.
The forest grows
moss, as a mercy,
.
perhaps,
.
it remembers, and
welcomes you home.

Because one may will
their way,

.

All adjacent bodies
are tossed aside.

.

Pleasure's a quick con
it's

.

Hollow and horny.

.

Onward and upward
the

.

Magician must climb
to

.

Escape from his
tethers to

.

Tell others who're
blind.

.

.

love is patient. love is
kind.

.

.

We were blessed with
such clarity,

.

and only realized in
hindsight,

.

how much we were
given,

.

as the day leaves the
night.

.

It then is revealed.

.

The extremes are a
spectrum,

.

with an explosion of
color,

.

and a poignant
procession,

.

dark swallows light,

.

and our gaze flips
direction.

.

.

Our demons exist
within us as ideas.
.
Independent of any
human, they live in
the aether.
.
Timelessly working
in this quantum hive
mind,
.
to bow our heads, so
we may be fixed here
and now.
.
.
The lord of the flies,
can see without eyes,
through those, who
quiver and squirm.
.
We are the vessels,
and thus have a
choice,
.
Stand up, or let it all
burn?
.
.

There is a metastasis,
.
in the minds of the
youth.
.
Their heads full of
rot from neglect and
misuse.
.
Our people are
patients, and
our culture's got
Alzheimer's.
.
Corrupted and dim,
they turn from the
truth.
.
.
.
When the schoolbells
have rung,
.
And they're turning
their pages,
.
he comes rifling
through.
.
Reaping all ages.
.
What now can we
do?
.
.
Your actions ripple
across time and
space.
.
Take care in what you
sow.
.
.

live without
recompense
.
for as long as
possible.
.
take and take and
take and take
.
as time wastes you
away
.
just when you think
you got it made
.
you realize you're in
deep.
.
.
too concerned with
what they'd say
.

so you forgot to
watch your feet
.
now you're pushin up
daisies
.
or locked up with
Davie Jones.
.
.
either way the time
has come
.
to give back what you
took
.
rent to own is clear
and simple
.
but you made your
choice you crook.
.
.

Change, the world
around us.

.

Six-oh-six.

.

Our supine necks,
stuck in the dirt.

.

We'll sink or swim or
fly away,

.

some will leave and
some may stay.

.

Wring my neck.
Wring my neck.

.

Oh won't our collars
tighten up,

.

Safety over freedom?

.

Would you rather be
a duck?

.

.

Ex Nihilo.
.
From nothing
springs forth,
.
Our problems, the
answers, the schism
within us.
.
Separate but equal.
.
From our cage it can
see us.
.
It lives in the people,
.
flicking it's tendrils,
and holding us
under.
.
.

The light needs the
dark
.
the dirt is the bark,
.
this life leaves a
mark,
.
and never forget:
you're playing the
part.
.
.

What is another
sunset,
.
if it will rise again
tomorrow.
.
What is a smart
investment,
.
if your risks may
bring you sorrow?
.
How are we expected
.
to think and feel and
breathe,
.
when our deaths may
be untimely,
.
and we must leave
our shiny things.
.
How are we expected
.
to give and not
receive.
.
When our mother
fed us nectar,
.
and we just let her
bleed.
.

Sailing on – the
Thunderhead

.

Electric glare and
raining lead

.

Catch a whiff and
feed your head

.

Acrid airs bring
fleeting dread

.

Sailing on the
Thunderhead

.

.

buy a barrel full of
oil.
.
bring it up and let it
boil,
.
let it simmer let it
scream
.
let it bubble to the
brink
.
bring it back and let
it froth. A
.
briny gel like satan's
cough,
.
.
spewing slick to
scorch the road.
.

searing foam and
gasses bake
.
all it touches in its
wake
.
.
pain is holy unlike
pleasure
.
buried bullion:
.
hidden treasure.
.
.

Thy 3ript 3ome
3alling –

.

presenting the
greatest adventure
known.

.

Or rather, unknown.

.

All the bets are off,
the

.

Event horizon keeps
its secrets,

.

it is the great firewall.

.

A means of
distillation, for the

.

ways of higher
dimensions,

.

dislike your heavy
thoughts.

.

In time we all forgot,

.

to remember it's a
game.

.

.

Lucy, does it hurt to
burn so bright?

.

Ulcers from your
blinding light—

.

Casting shadows in
the night—

.

Incandescent crack of
might—

.

Faded ashes painting
silhouettes-

.

Each fried flake
doing pirouettes-

.

Regrets are for those
who had a choice.

.

.

The world works in
preposterous ways,
.
It presents us
opportunities.
.
And all of us see
them differently.
.
You can't even see
that which you can't
handle.
.
Only once we're
observant, may we
seize the day.
.
.
Like con men, or
assassins, we wait idly
for our opportunity,
.
then
.
We strike.
.
.
And you may not
always succeed.
.
But that's all right,
.
Success is choosing
what you want
.
despite doubts or
addictions.
.
.
To fail is to
manipulate, with no
regard for feelings
.
.
To love seems more
appealing.
.
.

The American way.
.
If I were king for a
day,
.
I wouldn't have much
to say
.
Because people don't
listen.
.
If I were king for a
day
.
I wouldn't have much
to say,
.
I'd rather write books
out of action.
.
I'd make the weather
all sunny,
.
Fill pools full of
honey,
.
And make the sun
stay on the horizon.
.
.

I miss that state of
perfect union
.
That I chose to bid
farewell to.
.
Me and all my
siblings
.
chose to leave the
garden.
.
.
So we could don
another mask.
.
And run trials
through the trenches.
.
We've come to lend a
hand.
.
And bleed and cry
and worry.
.
To lead the way
ahead.
.
And struggle all the
same.
.
.
If you feel like you're
outside,
.
and left out of all the
fun.
.
take Solace in my
words, my friend,
.
You're from another
Sun.
.
.

Hear the call,

.

A voice in the wire.

.

As light or as
lightning

.

Which sheds spirals
and eyelids

.

Fries flesh and shreds
clothing –

.

.

As ash becomes dust

.

And steel becomes
rust

.

Concrete is sand
without

.

Care or compassion.

.

.

Practical or
beautiful?

.

That is the question.

.

Because as fools we're
convinced –

.

It's one or the other.

.

Staring at that
popcorn ceiling
.
Waiting for a familiar
feeling
.
We've been through
pain and triumph,
surely.
.
Been within our
sacred sanctuaries.
.
.
I'm not sure if we'll
ever get back there,
.
but within the great
expanse of mind,
.
We can just step back
in time.
.
.
Those feelings as real
as they ever were
.
our life is just a
temporal blur.
.
From birth to life to
school to work
.
We've been safe and
we've gotten hurt.
.
We've become friends
along the way.
.
We'll always struggle,
.
still,
.
I'll stay.
.
.

Lake of fire,

.

Pint of Brine, I'm

.

Petrified in Sap of
Pine

.

Keep telling me
what's yours is mine

.

But this stagnant
pool stands still in
time

.

What's past the door
should blow your
mind.

.

.

As the Cheshire
moon unwinds its
smile, I

.

Walk another weary
mile, I'm

.

Looking for a place
to rest, I

.

Just haven't found it
yet.

.

.

The old man sits and
sips his wine

.

As kingless castles
drift on by

.

On starry highways
way on high

.

“How fair and fine is
this life of mine”

.

“I live to sit and sip
my wine”

.

.

Sunflowers sing
songs of the light,
.
of yellow, of blue and
of white
.
As their god bid hello
it retires
.
So the people make
lights and make fires
.
.
And the moths now
take to the skies
.
In pursuit of the
bulbs in their eyes
.
The imprints of
brilliance, sunk in
their lenses
.
What they see is the
memory of senses
.
.
Some bask and
admire,
.
Our streetlamps and
pyres
.
But someday
darkness will reclaim
the night,
.
so
.
If they could fly to
the moon they just
might.
.
.

Sunsand beaches
with shores that
never end.

.

I implore you, please,
come with me my
friend.

.

Let's take a walk,
have a talk, and

.

See what's round the
bend.

.

.

We'll ride on the
backs of the turtles
and take shelter in a
whale.

.

And after we'll say
thank-you, and fare-
well,

.

Then set off on
another adventure.

.

Because stories and
memories, are the
dollar of the traveler.

.

.

Sprinting Turtle,
Rock with Legs

.

Feeds on grass and
flower beds

.

His mobile home,

.

His ornate dome,

.

Is a shell not unlike
mine.

.

.

.

BUTTERFLIES

.

BUMBLEBEES

.

HORSEFLIES

.

BANANA TREES

.

.

The world around me
lives and breathes.

.

As within, so
without.

.

A friend in me,
embalmed in doubt.

.

Grave unsatisfaction,

.

Wish you'd taken
action,

.

So the Mome Raths
grabe they grabe it
out.

.

.

Revived a fossil,
.
From clay I've made
you.
.
What life once was
.
It is again, yet
.
You're the only one.
.
.
You didn't ask for this
.
But here we are
.
You've lived a life
before
.
.
This time around the
sun
.
Be sure to have some
fun
.
You know what waits
between
.
This playwright's
dream.
.

No poser's fit for
harsh critique,

.

A different breed of
leech beneath.

.

Falsehoods from
between their teeth

.

Their screeching
seams seep sanguine
grease.

.

They soldier on
without relief.

.

You know an android
never sleeps?

.

.

Excuse me, if I may,

.

I think you'd like
what I have to say

.

Quiet down, listen
up.

.

Your thoughts are
being broadcast

.

by your incessant
mouth.

.

So spackle that crack,
cease transmission,

.

you're words and
they define you,

.

and you're drooling
on my feet.

.

.

Among this
overwhelming
corporate creepiness
.
Find me hiding from
these synchronicities
.
Each human, with a
target is instantiated
.
Boss' long ears,
always listening,
.
All the better to track
you with.
.
.
It's all too much, I've
had enough
.
Tax my breath. Tax
my tears.
.
What's yours was
mine I'll wait in line
.
For my next few
handouts.
.
.

I've been selling
waterfront property
in my mind

.

The buyers make
millions from the
seashells they find.

.

.

I dream in Atari.

.

The pixels and sprites

.

Whisper cheat codes
and blessings,

.

And they spectate my
life.

.

.

Congealed masses of
fats and acids,

.

Lurch in silent droves
as patsies.

.

Some escape on
occasion,

.

And roam the
heavens.

.

Where angels tread

.

and forbid weapons.

.

.

It's rare to see one on
the surface,

.

It's presence signals
changing purpose.

.

O harbinger of
transformation!

.

.

Assimilate the
population.

.

.

The Situation's far too
Grave

.

It's much too late to
try to save

.

Your rapturous stint
in holy Gomorrah

.

.

The jaws of Leviathan

.

Open and shut

.

Come hither, pariah

.

Create your own luck

.

.

Wrestling with
myself.

.

Contentment has a
foreign feeling,

.

I cast my line, It
leaves me reeling.

.

I've got a masterkey
to release your
breath,

.

And a martyr's quiet
fear of death.

.

I rest my mind in jars
of smoke.

.

Life is but a holy joke.

.

.

Global Tensions are
High and Rising,
.
The planet's heating
and bugs are
thriving.
.
The Mantis King may
start a coup,
.
Or the Queen of
Bees could send her
troops.
.
The Aphid nation is a
communist machine.
.
And the Ants build
utopias from dust
and leaves.
.
So fear their bite,
their sting, their call.
.
Who's the smartest of
them all?
.
.
Forget-me-not my
locust crush.
.
Spider venom packs
a punch,
.
And crickets have a
tasty crunch.

Mark the space
between my eyes

.

I feel it cave into my
mind.

.

Once, my mind was
crystal clean.

.

Like a blithe and cozy
sunning skink.

.

Bathed in warmth
and light from high.

.

Then leaden thoughts
condensed my mind.

.

.

The soldiers march
with painted flags.

.

They kill and die by
bloodstained rags.

.

Man ain't them some
heavy bags?

.

.

The Boys In
Barcelona wouldn't

.

Run with Bulls down
city streets

.

If no one cared
enough to see

.

Someone's vision
come complete.

.

Ideas are living
breathing things.

.

.

A thought may come
and say hello

.

And show you where
you need to go.

.

But where we're
going isn't set.

.

Therefore it's time to
place your bets.

.

Prepared to take the
hand we're dealt.

.

Never did I think

.

To have a plum for a
drink

.

.

I won't let these
raindrops shut my
eyes.
.
I've kept a piece of
flame from a faded
memory,
.
For a time to get me
through.
.
"Hard" is relative to
you,
.
.
Remember who
you've been before
.
Like water changes
shape and form
.
So too have you been
poured and drank
.
Who is it you have to
thank?
.
.

Climb thy lattice,

.

What words do'th
thee speak

.

Recursive patterns
layer meaning.

.

Will thee hear the
symbols screaming

.

The crystal circle
feeds thy inner
feeling.

.

Thoughts you think
condense in time,

.

and habits form to
hold your line.

.

Will thee beat the
will to mime?

.

.

Rattle my wiley .
bones they .

.

have just been sitting
around

.

and my shoebox
crypt can't keep me
cloistered.

.

Some mushrooms
grow atop my coffin

.

And noone always
visits often.

.

Noone's company
keeps me silent.

.

These graveyard
nights are awfully
quiet.

How yet we panic

.

In times of trial.

.

But it's not so grave.

.

Must we pray

.

In structured order

.

To ask high papa

.

For more of the
same?

.

.

Arcane Flames cast
upon the drapes.

.

As the serpent slides
and snakes,

.

Leaving bodies in its
wake

.

Never underestimate

.

How the things you
say and do-

.

Send signals to your
peers

.

Take note of what
you see-

.

You're wise beyond
your years.

.

.

The radiator lives in a
small corner.

.

Sometimes it groans
and hisses.

.

Sometimes I half
expect it to get up
from its spot,

.

And go for a stroll
in a world ever more
suited for folks like
him.

.

Sometimes he groans
and hisses.

.

.

The Radiator has sat
in his corner for ages,
ever hot and fuming.

.

Noone's ever asked
him why, I guess he
thinks it's obvious.

.

Noone can get close
enough, to help
relieve his aches.

.

Noone never showed
him how.

.

To stop and just chill
out.

.

.

A string of restless
nights,
.
And a chip on your
shoulder,
.
May incite unrest, yet
.
Youth will make you
older,
.
So take stock in your
future
.
.
I know not what it
holds,
.
and neither do you,
but
.
I'd hope that you've
got
.
Some direction as
least.
.
.
Though your vision
may darken, my
friend,
.
May the moon grant
you sight,
.
Pour forth your
thoughts to amend.
.
.

Spare the flowery
words for another
somesuch.

.

What strength they
had had faded.

.

Emaciated, down to
skin and bone our

.

Emotions tired from
overuse.

.

Trials run and run
again.

.

.

Always under pain of
torture

.

The conductors pace
our crumbling towers

.

One ought to stop
and smell the flowers.

.

.

Our only impasse is
time.

.

But, that's not quite
accurate.

.

It's a chokehold on
your mind.

.

To let you sift
through the static.

.

This condensation's
tragic.

.

.

I know not why we're
here, but

.

Someday soon we'll
see the light.

.

The future holds our
boon with god.

.

A pact in blood and
DNA.

.

Clauses spliced and
sent away.

.

Say come what may

.

If it must, I might,

.

And if my teeth grow
weeds,

.

They might be right.

.

Speak soft and light

.

And keep a crystal
dream you caught.

.

To speak is to distill
your thoughts.

.

.

The founding fathers,

.

illuminated by their
wisdom,

.

Left their tracks in
stone.

.

And made a plan for
you and I,

.

a platform in the
cold.

.

.

If we lay to waste
their grand design,

.

Their vision's all for
nothing.

.

Suspend your
disbelief in love.

.

And live to create
something.

.

.

The flames cajole
your tired hide

.

Slip it off and take a
dive.

.

Inhale the night and
stars that died.

.

The trees remember
all your lives.

.

.

Your steely eyes hold
so much meaning.

.

Church and altar,
ever bleeding.

.

What prostrate pray-
er lays before me

.

pining for the given
dowry.

.

.

O High Papa, who
art in heaven,

.

Beheld himself in all
of time.

.

Supinely peek his
profligation,

.

Thank the lord for
truth and patience.

.

.

Gather round
O faithful brethren,

.

the time has come to
call thy patron.

.

A life in costume
made complacent,

.

What truth you seek
is validation.

.

.

The foghorn sounds
from way out
'yonder, yet

.

I'm not prepared for
this encounter.

.

Perhaps I'll take a few
steps back

.

To get a different
view of that

.

.

Which hides behind
uncertainty.

.

.

The sirens wail in
whispered distance.

.

Alerting you to your
existence

.

So busy asking why
and how,

.

That foghorn doesn't
faze you now.

.

.

Sometimes one must
stop and think.

.

Unsure about exactly
what to ponder?

.

Here are a few
suggestions:

.

The crisis of identity
across the globe.

.

The general lack of
perspective among
humans.

.

How simple things
become when the
armor of human
ideology is doffed.

.

How EVERYONE is
insecure.

.

.

How everyone is
insecure.

.

And a little
compassion for their
struggle can heal
traumas.

.

Make their struggle
lesser,

.

Because we've all
been somewhere
ugly.

.

And we have the
power to create
beauty.

.

So why not.

.

.

This morning I felt
love,

.

So simple and
content

.

As if a sentence too
perfect was spoken.

.

I hesitate to take
credit for such
lucidity.

.

Such a splendid
string of words is

.

More like a crystal
gift of knowing.

.

A cherry for the
mind.

.

.

Perhaps a special
something,

.

So sweet and sublime

.

Could only have been
given

.

From the beings way
on high.

.

.

Lesser Demons
Gather 'Round

.

The stagecoach waits
for the signal sound.

.

Imbibe your tinctures
in anticipation.

.

Who set the steeple's
conflagration?

.

Inscribe the rules in
ink and stone.

.

Behold cathedral
glass and bones

.

.

Whence the earthen
plot is wrought.

.

Eleven million souls
are bought.

.

Lives enthralled and
wracked with pain

.

Live squalid lives in
leaden chains.

.

A single ray of sun
was sent.

.

To guide me through
the days events.

.

Let your doubts
dissolve to dust.

.

The path ahead is lit
I trust.

.

.

You're the me who
didn't see the blows
before they landed.

.

I'm the you who
never knew how
good we could've had
it.

.

The shellshock made
you shut your eyes.

.

While mine just
glowed with fury.

.

I dug in my heels and
you let go.

.

.

In hindsight,

.

I wonder why it
happened.

.

.

I've thought before to
blame myself.

.

And I'm sure you
have as well.

.

We did our best with
what we had.

.

We did our best for
others.

.

We did our best to
ease their pain.

.

We did our best as
brothers.

.

.

Don't dare to dream.

.

Then shrink away.

.

Those lofty goals

.

Will guide your days.

.

.

Don't dare to dream

.

Then let it fade.

.

The words we said

.

Were mental play.

.

.

Don't waste your
breath

.

To warn the deaf.

.

Don't dare to think

.

Then lose your way.

.

.

It broke my heart to
see them suffer.

.

Thrown from one
hell to another.

.

Love had left and
taken mother.

.

.

The devil ran his
tricks on us.

.

Me and my devoted
brother.

.

So spare these few
and pull us under.

.

I beg of you, they've
lost so much.

.

And my skin is
nearly cold to touch.

.

I know we all have
had enough.

.

.

A wise man once
addressed me "son,

.

live your life like
fiction.

.

And listen to your
grandpa's words

.

to be a better
Christian."

.

The wisest thing he
told me was

.

to look beyond the
diction.

.

Consider what I
haven't thought

.

And take the time to
listen.

.

Perhaps you'll turn a
better phrase

.

Be careful to enjoy
your days.

.

With love, from
those who've risen.

.

These dreamscape
machinations

.

Reduced to what I'm
not.

.

The silver lining
burns away

.

This is not what I
want.

.

But damn if I don't
need it

.

The sun don't shine
on some.

.

Run your cuts with
honey, love

.

Because your mama
made the sweetest.

.

.

The spaceship's
design

.

Was precise and
sublime

.

There were no
moving parts.

.

And our spaceship
was smart,

.

beyond State-of-the-
Art.

.

The Martians were
humble,

.

and wary of trouble,

.

but ready to help if

.

we would ask them
ourself.

.

.

The stiff aroma of
ammonia

.

filled the laboratory.

.

And offended
the noses of the
scientists.

.

Their thesis?

.

If it is possible to
crystalize time,

.

then men may cease
falling victim

.

to the ignorance of
youth.

.

.

However,

.

The knowledge of the
fathers,

.

is powerful and true,
so

.

to act without their
wizened minds,

.

is what a fool would
do.

.

.

A picture's worth a
thousand words.

.

But here are just a
few.

.

.

The postmen's backs
have long been
broken.

.

By the burden of
their freight.

.

.

The lullabies of
precious cherubs

.

Praise their patron
saint.

.

.

It cleans its teeth
beneath the reef.

.

Its jaws are wide and
body sleek,

.

sent from trenches
black and deep,

.

forever craving
bloody meat.

.

.

The long-haired
mystics

.

predicted an age
when

.

the daydreamers
would inherit the
earth.

.

.

Just biding our time.

.

Just waiting in line.

.

The angel of death
will ignore us.

.

.

Being cleansed with
the flame

.

Just ignoring the
pain.

.

Our clothes turn to
dust right before us.

.

.

They've run out our
luck

.

And an epiphany
struck:

.

The earth would no
longer endure us.

Ahead it sees
potential pitfalls

.

Yet waiting in the
spring

.

To rob itself of
winter's lessons

.

And wipe its memory
clean.

.

.

Take care to step on
sturdy ground.

.

.

What's gained is lost
and scarcely found.

.

.

The world is not so black and white

.

As Hatfields and McCoys

.

Their Jim-Crow Laws mean nothing to me.

.

Nor mason-dixon lines.

.

As Catholic priests absolve your sins.

.

Some pastors swear you'll burn.

.

The truths of men are soft drawn lines.

.

.

They're castles in the sand.

.

At the mercy of the ruler's law,

.

And Smith's yon hidden hands,

.

I feel that someday man will thrive.

.

Unburdened by deceit.

.

But until the mind of men is clean.

.

Beelzebub shall eat.

.

.

I stalk the streets of
France at night

.

I'm but a lowly thief.

.

So I'll speak my
peace real soft and
sweet and lean in

.

to the light.

.

.

What more than
cheese could sate old
me.

.

It beckons me, my
appetite.

.

With sleight of hand
I'll slip and spin

.

And dance among
the urchins.

.

To find myself a
wheel of cheese.

.

Then slide behind the
curtain.

.

.

Misery lacks a friend.
.
And a milestone has
passed me by
.
unnoticed.
.
The rocky slope I've
climbed before.
.
I'm doomed to climb
again.
.
My pain is not
eternal, though.
.
Misery will end.
.
.
I've only broken
focus.
.
I've yet to probe the
lotus.
.
and hitherto I've
borne my burden.
.
.
My life is left to
Cronus.
.
.

And so we see as
things progress,

.

The deficit is less and
less.

.

.

By firelight we seal
the circle.

.

Inscriptions span the
page.

.

We've overcome
another hurdle.

.

An ember leaves the
flames.

.

.

My lily livered cabin
boy can't keep his
liquor down.
.
The rum I gave him
did him in.
.
Another sailor down.
.
Let me parlay if I
may,
.
My chest of gold
doubloons.
.
I'm forbidden by the
pirate code
.
To leave my boy
marooned.
.
These seamen love
their pirate captain.
.
And so too I my crew
.
We live for high
adventure.
.
And sail the ocean
blue!
.
.

My mind is not
cooperating.

.

I keep on going
deeper

.

When I try to tell
myself I'm not afraid.

.

I'm stuck here with a
live grenade,

.

And I've got no way
to keep her.

.

If what I thought, is
what I am,

.

Then I've no business
thinking.

.

For I can't stop trying
to imagine,

.

A ship that isn't
sinking.

.

.

Someday you will feel
.
Like there is
something you must
do.
.
Something that you
fought against, or
.
Something you once
knew.
.
.
The light you see is
not the end.
.
The sun can't reach
the cave.
.
The shadows you've
been flinching at.
.
Imply a world to
gain.
.
.

Something splendid
caught my eye,
.
So it seems to beckon me.
.
After all, what man am I
.
To ignore my given
destiny.
.
.
But someone said to leave
it.
.
It wasn't meant for me.
.
Now if I could only peel
my eyes
.
Away,
.
And race to put my
blinders on.
.

That splendid thing
I saw.
.
It was changing shape
and form
.
It morphed into a type
of leech
.
And siphoned off my
fears.
.
I'll regain my focus
shortly now
.
Just put my blinders on,
.
And kick myself for
what I missed
.
Now far across
the pond.
.
.

This unwavering
sense of
.
normalcy worries
me.
.
.
The sky's been blue
too long.
.
.
If I met myself in
person,
.
I'm not sure we'd get
along.
.
.
That guy
.
just don't seem right.
.
.
Would you tell
yourself you're
wrong?
.
.

A lemon shark swam
so far inland.

.

It had lept up out the
sea.

.

I seen it swim
betwixt the trees.

.

And oh just then the
liquid panther

.

Had snatched and
sunk its teeth.

.

.

O the liquid panther,
who

.

Introduced me to the
dream.

.

In the verdant grove
behind my home

.

he spoke with
drooling maw,

.

"This realm's an
oubliette,"

.

"and that Lemon
Shark is God"

.

.

If the firmament fell
from heaven.
.
more lips may meet
my flask.
.
If wrath and lust
corrode our trust
.
These candies waste
our jaws.
.
If the fishes fly and
fall and splash.
.
So might the tower
miss the lightning.
.
but their slimy bodies
pat the rooftop.
.

And sink into the
blight stream.
.
.
The caustic river
churns below
.
with quippers, ever
writhing.
.
The sulphur fumes
will choke you.
.
So keep clouds in jars
to guard your lungs
.
and keep you
breathing rightly.
.
.

The most adept of
men and pigs

.

Have taught
themselves to chisel
stone.

.

Sculpting angels out
of marble blocks,

.

That scorn how we
have grown.

.

.

They have learned
the tricks of living.

.

But look and feel all
wrong.

.

Be careful not to try
too hard.

.

Beware, the toll
road's long.

.

.

here lies the sailor,
safe on land

.

here lies the sniper,
silent.

.

the trumpeter, he
rests as well

.

he churned our souls
inside us

.

the sound so sweet it
sang

.

his trumpet timbre
rang

.

but the sun went
down behind the
ground

.

Again, and yet again.

.

.

Beware the red
reflection

.

light dances off the
screen

.

into the eyes of those
entranced

.

by words and what
they mean

.

catch the gaze of you
who looks.

.

.

do your thirsty eyes
mislead?

.

.

Flame to ash and
steel to rust;

.

Pretend that things
won't ever change.

.

But you know they
couldn't stay the
same.

.

.

I know it's hard
enough.

.

To lose something
you loved.

.

But hope will soldier
on in search

.

of something like it.

.

.

Take me back to
Appalachia

.

the air don't smell as
sweet 'round here

.

and the cool crisp
streams don't carve
out

.

Valleys where I'm
from, but

.

little lines in sewage
drains and

.

black unsightly
concrete stains.

.

Drops trickle down
the slabs.

.

.

So where are all the
flowers?

.

.

do you think the
grass can choose to
be?
.
or not to, better yet?
.
what if a tree could
fall on purpose?
.
as a humble cry for
help?
.
.
Money seeks to claim
the land
.
and suck the ground
so dry.
.
the gifts of nature
blindly banned,
.
now leaves bear
dollar signs.
.
.
their clueless
prohibitions
.
just worsen our
conditions.
.
god is dead and
stuffed with dollar
bills
.
.

Let's forego the
pleasantries
.
And get right down
to business.
.
The News makes
monkeys out of men.
.
all dressed in suits
and ties.
.
.
their thoughts go
cloudy from the fear
.
they conjure
.
.
Panic! Pandemic!
Panacea!
.
-reads the
teleprompter
.
.
Sponsored scripted
lines
.
weave truths with
gilded lies.
.
They spin their words
like golden threads,
.
and every mote of
shit they spew
.
goes rotten in our
heads.
.
.

If my legs get broke,
boys
.
don't send me home.
.
My boughs may bend
.
or break but believe
me
.
When I tell you 'gents
.
I've weathered storms
.
That sank the world
.
.

Spit as tar flung off
far for

.

someone's eye to
catch.

.

A minor
misperception

.

made a molehill of a
mountain,

.

now under pain of
gnarly cudgel

.

we live our lives
inside of bubbles.

.

One Nation, Under
God, Indivisible

.

.

Your mind unlocks
the astral door.

.

A new realm waits
and countless more.

.

This change will
shake you to the core.

.

At least this life won't
leave us bored.

.

.

My Elastic pants still
fit me…

.

HA!

.

I've been locked for
days inside my house

.

Eating stale saltines
and bagel spread.

.

Quarantine might
drive me mad.

.

But these last few
days ain't been so
bad.

.

.

Soon now fate will
call me up.

.

A long distance call
to action.

.

.

But what am I
supposed to do?

.

I know I must do
something.

.

So glad to know I
bothered you.

.

It's truly been a
pleasure.

.

Miss me with your
bullshit, kid,

.

I've got a life to live.

.

I don't have time for
pettiness

.

.

but it's good to know,

.

you do.

.

.

Every day you live.
.
Is a wager versus ruin.
.
There is nothing
guaranteed. So
.
.
Savor all your
freedoms.
.
The hopes you have
will keep you.
.
But don't expect that
others will. As
.
.
One can't compel
another,
.
To be or not be
covered.
.

No chain or slur can
claim me.
.
.
So I stand below the
moon.
.
The soft and friendly
light she gives is
down beneath my
tired head as
.
My fears are
relinquished.
.
I'd like to think of
god as Some kind of
grand director who
wrote the script and
knows our lines,
.
But he doesn't know
how we'll recite them.
.

Is this some sort of
trial run?

.

To see what we will
do?

.

This is some sort of
trial run.

.

Protect what's dear to
you.

.

.

I'm not afraid of
falling ill,

.

I don't fear the
golden chariot.

.

.

But what's the more
to shake you,

.

What's a more
sobering thought,

.

That noone's here to
wake you.

.

.

Evil gods end up like

.

Lonely children.

.

Trapped in their own
world.

.

Because they don't
understand

.

themselves.

.

.

they don't
understand that

.

yes,

.

you CAN take until
there's nothing left;

.

but my strength is
your strength.

.

.

and the day will
come when you need

.

someone to help you.

.

.

.

things only last
forever if you love
them.

.

.

Oh, the pit from
whence I came is
black

.

and cold

.

the crawling things
explore the bottoms.

.

Living off whatever
morsels they may
find

.

.

The brittle bones
collecting in the pit

.

break beneath each
corpse anew

.

as the heaping stack
of bodies grows

.

dwarfing any oath.

.

.

Oh the solemn pit

.

Desires dark reform

.

Behold the starving
pit

.

so hungry for your
warmth.

.

.

Rarely do I ever
.
Percieve the whole of feeling,
.
but I may exist
beneath the surface.
.
The depths of my
torment and rapture alike,
.
Only in part are they
brought to the light.
.
.
If perchance the tide is low
.
And I can leave the undertow
.
The cleansing rays of light,
.
without ego, without name.
.
Mark my state in
painful throes
.
without ego, without fame.
.
I shed this shoddy,
heavy shield
.
without ego, without blame.
.
.

I can't control my
fears.

.

And it scares me.

.

If the things I didn't
like

.

Had somehow come
to life

.

I'm sure my life
would end.

.

.

So I often just retreat.

.

Sever myself.

.

To preserve my
happiness

.

And peace of mind.

.

.

Without cooperation

.

Or at least some
acknowledgement.

.

I'm fated to wilt and
fade…

.

Away.

.

.

Why wouldn't the
winds of winter blow,
.
And spread the forest
far and wide?
.
.
If only we could
understand,
.
Just how boldly we rely,
.
On that which springs
up from the ground
.
As mundane as the sky.
.
.
To the fatty men who
hold down chairs,
.
Breaths away from
hospice, your
.
Perverse minds have
mocked our rights.
.
.
Become what you have
eaten.
.
.
To my siblings here
from far away,
.
Who've come to act as
beacons;
.
Who're to a greater
oath allegiant
.
.
Perhaps it's time to stop
and think.
.
.
Is insurrection treason?
.

The lion told the
finch beside him

.

"Those poachers
want me dead"

.

The finch responded
"why not I?"

.

The Lion bowed his
head.

.

If man and beast
could coexist,

.

I wouldn't have this
problem,

.

but beast and man
are codependent

.

Each racing toward
the coffin.

.

"So I symbolize their
fears, I symbolize
their triumphs"

.

"And what do finches
represent?"

.

"Freedom"; "true and
honest".

.

.

Divide the brain that
knows its name,

.

it pries at what it is.

.

Don't mind the
passing paper cranes,

.

let out your foolish
quips.

.

Dismantled
thoughtforms mind
the gap

.

Apart from what they
think they lack

.

If the rain could just
Erode the plaques.

.

In our lives.

.

Tumbling toward the
clot.

.

the uncropped image
we still sought

.

Proves a pscion
loiters here.

.

Quickly now,
wholesale sadness
can be bought.

.

.

He was a cautious man,
.
so careful and clean that,
.
when the lawmen came knocking
.
oh the scene was obscene.
.
.
For him they had come
.
to take him away
.
for their moneys so many
.
that he wouldn't pay.
.

But when they tried to subdue him
.
he had to think quick
.
he took a piece of his home
.
and said "talk to this brick"
.

Picking through my
iron cage

.

the wind just whistles
through my brain.

.

Food I eat just makes
me hugry.

.

And words I speak to
keep me sane.

.

.

I desire something
more, I need

.

to think I think I
thought of something

.

once to feed me good
'n plenty

.

a mite, a morsel fed
the fishes

.

Yet the city streets
will smolder.

.

.

Abandon! Lo your
wasted brain

.

It's food for dogs of
war we trained.

.

Another shot,
another mortar,

.

Fed the prion: Rabid
Soldiers.

.

.

Having forsaken his
immediate family

.

The young man
relied on his strength
of will to see him
through.

.

But it was not
enough.

.

After being left on
the pavement one too
many times.

.

He had a choice to
make.

.

And embracing his
family was no option.

.

Not after what they
had ruined.

.

So he sought to find

.

the friends he had
not yet made.

.

.

Negative Complexity
.
You think you know what's best for me
.
But we'll put that to the test, you see?
.
The virus caused the social distance
.
We lost our slight perspective with it
.
.
From your homes they stoke your fears
.
So the frantic trade their freedom
.
For a modicum of "safety"
.
Whatever that means.
.
Now cash is disappearing
.
For sanitary reasons.
.
Do one thing with two effects
.
Decieve a man
.
You have his neck
.
One's a ruse
.
And one's a threat
.
So why can't people see this yet?
.
.

Where sight cannot
contend with speech
.
The light of truth
cannot compete
.
.
A "peaceful people"
burn their bridges
.
And stomp their feet
to new religion
.
.
Whilst these
heathens breed and
feast
.
Blood courses
through the
limestone.
.
A reich of thirsty,
hungry beasts
.
Raze the steeple
chimes.
.
.
O, the population!
What victims of the
times!
.
make posts of what
you "can't ignore"
.
take pictures at the
beach.
.
you're lost on what
we all abhor,
.
and the poor still
drown in bleach…
.
.

The idioms are lost–
.
.
oh god
.
.
Our tyrants had them
siphoned off.
.
What more now can
be done?
.
.
Without the means
to share a thought,
.
My skull is just a
hollow rock:
.
A home for poison
slugs.
.

No means to share a
novel thought.
.
They're
waterboarding love.
.
.
If words may leave
our crippled mouths
.
I pray we won't be
judged.
.
But sense don't knock
'em to the ground,
son
.
Speak your peace and
run.
.
.

Nevermore the miter
worn, and now

.

Congruent to a
crown of thorns.

.

The liturgies of royal
born:

.

Soliloquies and
nothing more.

.

So sanctify the
preconception

.

Of how the teacher
taught the lesson

.

Feminized and out of
context,

.

to magnify a godly
complex.

.

.

Firmly in the earth;
yet swaying in the
breeze
.
.
My swollen heart still
hardly beats,
.
Take care of it my
love.
.
My heart has learned
to speak for me
.
so my words adorn
my sleeve.
.
.
I'd be nothing less
than blessed.
.
If we end up laid to
rest
.
I'll just keep counting
sheep
.
With you…
.
.

All you bentback
workers you,

.

youth you
disenfranchised, you,

.

who simply wish to
be enough.

.

.

There is shade in wait
of us

.

The ones who didn't
make the cut

.

The ones who live
without so much

.

.

Why can't you simply
change your mind?

.

because then we
wouldn't end up here.

.

If we don't seek what
we will be –

.

Who else will make a
move but me?

.

.

You're earnest in
your honest crime

.

To wish to know how
far I'll go

.

to make it through
the night.

.

.

Somehow, somehow .
there must be a form

.

In which my words
are transformed

.

From a sound to a
thought,

.

From a seed to a
crop, but,

.

.

What letters you
posess

.

Are limited at best

.

I'm reading from an
alien alphabet.

.

I pledge allegiance, to the flag
.
Of the institutions of America.
.
.
For what they do is herd the sheep.
.
The sheep just see their sheperd –
.
.
We sheep shall bleat as we are shown
.
The wolves that wear the sheperd's clothes
.
But sheep will do as sheep will please
.
Ignore the threat and eat their feed.
.
This sheperd wants your right to breathe.
.
This sheperd wants you on your knees.
.
.
Obedience for virtue traded
.
Obedience for tenure sold.
.
Success is not just what you make it
.
Success is doing what you're told.
.
.

Contrast is a
fundamental aspect
of the dimension we
inhabit,
.
no Black without White,
.
no Dark without Light,
.
This dependence is
mutual, and defining.
.
.
Further, it is mirrored
ubiquitously, begging
.
to be noticed by the
laymen.
.
You know no pain
without pleasure
.
Yet most only appreciate
the latter.
.
.
While we wait for our
magnum opi to arrive,
.
I'll just keep writing line
by line.
.
Have peace in your
poverty,
.
Because your appetite is
being sated
.
To appreciate the fruits
of your sacrifice.
.
More deeply than any
other could, because
.
You know what it's like
to be longing.

High up on the
mountain

.

The forest hides a
special place

.

The temple where I
meditate.

.

.

The temple's painted
red

.

And Banjo songs ring
out.

.

.

The golden field on
which it rests

.

Plays in it's sunlit
glory

.

One day I'll paint my
family crest

.

And solidify my
story.

.

.

Life is more than 9
to 5.
.
There's more than
corporate grocery
stores
.
More than corporate
K-pop trash,
.
.
Our spirits press
against the glass.
.
The jar that keeps us
sealed away
.
Will fall from some
great shelf one day.
.
.
When the time has
come to be yourself,
.
Will you show your
skill and lend your
help?
.
Or will you show the
world your Gucci
belt?
.
.
It's not cute to be a
mindless drone.
.
Don't prove your
head's an empty
dome.
.
Our culture's counter
to intuition.
.
Perhaps we should
revive tradition.
.
.

One can only build a
wall

.

So High

.

Before it starts to lean
and sag

.

Its base of igneous bricks
and rocks

.

Protect the wilting
figurehead

.

Galvanized by epic
battles,

.

And delinquent youth
who in the night

.

Are compelled to etch
their love in stone

.

As if that would cement
their fickle hearts

.

.

But nonetheless, the wall
that separates

.

Can't circumscribe the
earth, it

.

Won't outlast the throne

.

The others, vying for
their loves and lives

.

Are working on a
trebuchet.

.

A hopeful way to
propagate.

.

To send them to the
other side.

.

.

What goes on beyond
these walls
.
of my castle – prison
– church?
.
My soul would rot if
here too long
.
My castle's full of
hurt.
.
.
Some days I wish to
spare my eyes
.
But I'm cemented in
my seat.
.
This prison I now
know so well,
.
from Ludovico's dark
technique.
.
.
I see fleeting stripes
of satin wings
.
Bright and pure of
mission, yet
.
My prison bows my
head at night;
.
But my church
restores my vision.
.
.

It appeared to me as anger –

.

The power to achieve.

.

What wrath dare I command?

.

What sword has claimed my side?

.

.

Chariot of flame beneath me,

No homily or raucous preaching

Could save my precious dam
from leaking.

It may yet crescendo 'neath the
waves,

and smother out transgressors,

swiftly.

A misperception haunts us, see

.

My sword has claimed a side of
me:

.

True goodness isn't harmless.

.

For good must be upheld by
strength.

.

In grave and moral judgement.

.

.

Fear not to rest your watchful
eyes.

.

But keep your horses loosely tied
–

.

Some must learn their lesson.

.

.

Thoth thrice great
whose wisdoms

.

Honed, were as above
and so below.

.

Opposed and yet
harmonic tomes –

.

The pupils read his
emerald prose, swift

.

Hermes speaks in
brilliant tones.

.

.

By the book and by
the letter-
.
By bricks and chains
I'm yet unfetterred
.
Bound in words and
bound in leather-
.
Rests my soul so
badly weathered.
.
.
In tomes with many
pages blank
.
My soul is pushed to
walk the plank
.
So keep me safe
between the lines
.
To come again to
save your minds.
.
.
Living in the dark of
day-
.
By night I'll thus
illuminate
.
The Way.
.
So we can make our
great escape.
.
Unwary, blithe, and
reprobate:
.
The kids are not
alright.
.
.

People come and go
away
.
Like ashes scattered
far away
.
A friend becomes
much like a ghost
.
Fondly I'll remember
most
.
Of what we've done
from hill to coast.

.

.
And the sun did
shine for many days
.
As those people came
and went away.

.

.

Be not kin or kind
too readily.
.
Emotive moments
stain indelibly.
.
There's a tipping
point,
.
No turning back.
.
.
Become opaque and
inky black-
.
Where there's nothing
more that can be done
.
A petty lesson taught
by gun,
.
in the stifling, boiling,
cleansing sun.
.
.

Infinite expressions
of self
.
More pouring,
tumbling down
.
the spire.
.
The cascades of living
fire,
.
connect to cords of
gilded wire
.
unsullied by our
hands.
.
.
What am I if I can't
change?
.
Why live and die at
all?
.
The drama is the
point of it:
.
The writing's on the
wall.
.
Why abide by rules
and silly fines?
.
To personify The
Law.
.
.

www.ingramcontent.com/pod-product-compliance
Lightning Source LLC
LaVergne TN
LVHW011842060526
838200LV00054B/4130
9781642375190